Vacating

Denelle Black

Illustration by Nahlah Alsree

Vacating

Cover and illustration by Nahlah Alsree

For art enquires @Nahlx_

For you, **yes** you

When you feel alone,
in a room full of people.
I'm here
To remind you,
you are never alone.
Plus,
you have me,
The girl who wished she'd had light in her
darkness.

For, my Granddad

Edward Shakespeare

Who passed away 13 years ago this month.

I hope you're proud of me.

I love you,

As much as all the sweets

You let the fat me eat

Airborne

It's only right that I take this time to welcome you on board. I'm allowing you to come on board, which is one of the best decisions I'll make. They say when you are nervous, picture everyone else around you naked. But this is me. Naked. Bare. And open right in front of you

I have found myself, but I am still learning myself. Step by step, like A, B, C and 1, 2, 3. The last 2-3 years have been filled with happiness, sadness, magic, breaking, loving and strength, all wrapped into one. I've learnt what it is like to really be alone, to really be inside of yourself and be in silence. I've had to figure out that even if I do love with my whole heart, that doesn't mean the receiver must feel the same. They are not obligated to feel the same as me, just because I myself is feeling it. So in that sense I have also been selfish. Not everyone who comes along will leave, and this is something that I honestly didn't understand the meaning of until recently. Some do stay, and some do care

You see, when you get let down so much you don't see new people coming along as something good. You see it as bad because then, you'll start counting down the days in your head or on your fingers, of when they will leave you. Not wanting them to leave of course, but having the thought in your mind that this is what happens, so what is stopping it from happening all over again

There have been times, I have shut out the world. Switched off the lights, and placed a 'NOT HOME' sign on myself and stayed within the darkness. Subconsciously wishing for better. Not knowing better can only come from me, when I am willing to let it. No time before and no time after. I needed to actually write this from the heart and not just say that I would do so, because that is a big difference. Every page holds my sacred thoughts. There have been quite a number of situations that have not deserved my attention, but have received the most attention from me. As if I was addicted to loving the things that would sooner or later destroy me, and then mistake the destroying for something else. I think this is why I stay so long in toxic places. Out of the hope that they would change naturally

I would make excuses for peoples lack of commitment to knowing me and understanding me, to the fact that not everyone is the same and this is just how some people are. Instead of looking at it straight on and seeing first hand what was happening. Yes, it does hurt when you'd go above and beyond for people, for them to not even want to cross the bridge for you but, it's your responsibility to see this for what it is and know what you need to do next. No, the answer is not always to leave either. I had to understand that my moods could change in the split of a second and then go back to normal after an hour or so, as if nothing had just happened. I had to learn to be patient with my own self and take things slowly. I am human and I feel like I forget this at times

I have spent so much time invested in everything negative, that has happened, that when positive comes along, I never know, how to really take it on and act on it. I have pretended to be happy, just so I'm not asked about my problems because we all have them. I never wanted mine to be highlighted. I have pretended with so many of my emotions but never on love, I have never pretended on my love for anything or anyone. It was then that I started to embrace every single emotion that I felt, instead of blocking it out or hiding it away or shying away from it. I want to show you naked truth, ugly truth, bitter truth. My truth. What has broken me, and how everything that happens will make me stronger. I hope everything that happens to you will make you stronger and wiser. You are magical and your power is to continue being who you are. I thought I was someone, they never looked at twice. So I started to portray that. I've had panic attacks caused by stress of wanting to be perfect, instead of wanting to be exactly who I am

The hurt is not the end, it can be the beginning and most times the middle. Never the end. There has been birth, death, illness and all the in-betweens, which all make up what life is. Things happen and I had to let them happen instead of trying to prevent them or change them. Like certain situations I've tried to prevent and wished I could have stopped, things I wish I could have seen earlier. This is where I would become stuck, dwelling on what I could have changed instead of seeing this as an opportunity to now change

I realised wishing wasn't what I needed to do. I needed to pray. So I started, praying for myself. Praying for the sad, praying for the happy. Praying for my friends, for my family. For anyone close to my heart. I prayed for them individually. So I guess I will now pray for you all and your wellbeing and your courage and your hearts. There's more than just an aching heart, and along the way I have learnt this. It doesn't just end in the sadness, it's where you begin to realise, there are situations you think you won't overcome and then you sort of just get on with it and overcome them. You can do it, and you can face the demons and you can become the person you hope you can be. That person inside of you, is waiting to come out and face the world. You have to stop covering that person, you have to stop preventing yourself from blossoming and thinking it's you protecting yourself. You are only blocking your blessings this way. I want you to shine. I want you to become the best version of yourself that you can be. You have to be willing to let this occur

I'm letting you into a world, my wonderland, my safe place. Please come on board carefully, get comfy. There may be a bit of turbulence but you'll be safe, I promise. If you're alone, I am alone, we can be alone together. Please hold on tight and stay strapped in

Denelle Black xx

Flight plan

Take off 13

Climb 49

Cruise 91

Descent 141

Landing 207

God knows where he is taking you. Don't be scared of the stairs that appear in front of you."

take off

Story time

You do know you have every right
To tell your story, to make it clear
Do not feel as if you have to hide parts
Because of other people. Fuck other people
And their opinions
Stay true to your damn self
And tell your story

11A

You strap me in, I'm unable to move.

Is it just you and me here?

It feels like it.

Ready for take off?

No care, where we are off to,

Or end up.

Anywhere with you next to me,

Is a place I want to be

Enough

I am a night warrior

and a day lover

I know I am enough

Touched or untouched

I am so enough at times

no one knows how to handle it

I have always been enough

We both know it

I am enough

I am enough

I am enough

Trouble

When daisies started growing in my lungs. I was in trouble. I knew. I was in a lot of trouble. I decided to water them daily instead of cutting them down. My field is full of flowers trapped in my lungs now

Flowers

Those who like flowers pick them

Those who love flowers water them

This is the difference

The C word

I hate it, every morning your first sip is coffee. Wanting a taste from you became a secret habit of mine. I'm jealous of the way your lips hover over the mug

Hand pressed into your hip, I watch as you breathe in its scent. Almost like its compulsory for you. I'm addicted to what I couldn't stand in the beginning

You can't seem to go without your daily doses. I did hate coffee, I promise. Just not when it had anything to do with you. I knew what it did for you, and I just wanted to be your coffee

Learning your...

I want to know your habits, what makes your lip twitch, when you're angry? Does it even twitch when you're angry? Do you get angry?

What makes your heart skip beats? What makes your heart rate pick up such speed? I want all of your habits to become imprinted into my mind. What are the flaws you secretly try to hide?

Let them out, let me witness them. Show me the things you try to hide away from this world. The raw outcome of you, let me heal those pieces of your heart. If there are unfixed pieces, I want to learn you

Inside and out, because I want to help you

A Show

You are a show,

the type that I could watch on repeat

over and over again

Just like the sun when it sets

You are a show,

the type I could never forget

Speech

My voice smiles

My cheeks heat up

My lip quivers,

and all you do is open your mouth

His Better Love

That, let's pretend it's just a hit and run type. I've got no insurance for you...but this much I do assure you. I've got that better love. Rose petals on the floor, candles and champagne, romantic kind of love

The uncertainty of tomorrow makes me certain, of where I'd rather be today. Here. For the sweet nectarous juices you spill, like we're on a tropical island. Sun blazing, I promise, I'll do whatever it takes to get you to that place

While I feast on you, like you're the last supper, and your flower is like the ocean. Calling the lords name in vain, while I go down under like were visiting Australia. I fill your mind with enchanting thoughts

Let me strike this brush against your naked canvas, and paint a beautiful picture. I've got a good stroke come and be my Mona Lisa, allow me to really capture this moment in all it's glory

As soon as I'm finished, allow me to step back and admire the masterpiece that is you. I'll be everything you need; the painter, the exhibitionist and the art collector. Just so you can realise what you are really worth

3 words

"Have you eaten?"

"Have you gotten home safe?"

It had nothing to do with me. It is everything to do with, who you are, what you stand for. My eyes have noticed the plasters, the scars and even the blood designed in them. Yet I'm still here superglued, to the same spot. Unmoved and completely understanding

"This song reminds me of you?"

"What do you want to watch?"

"I got this for you?"

I love you has nothing to do with me, It's always been you

Selfless

I'm so selfless with my heart

Maybe that's why I gave you so much of it

That might be why I opened up a walkway

Just with your name on it

And it has two floors

For whenever you wanted to stay over

And make a home out of it

You will never know I loved

My body, it's an atlas. I have you travelling to all destinations within. The mind, the skin, the lips, your passport has been stamped out with me all over it. With every place you've visited. This red beating element we have inside of us. The electrical impulse, travelling down a special path

Tracing finger tips along me as if drawing out a map, or maybe the map is me. The device to finding your next step, needing me to get you there

You'll go on the roads, the pavements, the streets, but do I ever cross it? Do you see a lamp post and remember how much I loved the lights? You will never know I loved, but on the stars I do. As they glide through the futuristic sky, passing all the light years. Exploding as supernovae. Two different places seeing the same elements of the night sky

The intellectual information that seeped out of you was aspiring. Knowing factors people didn't even think twice about. Some didn't even think about it once. You will never know I loved but, on the books we explore I do. All the information we let soak into our brains, like rain on my favourite denim. Thinking ourselves out of basic knowledge could have been an obvious factor

You may never know I loved, but on these words you will feel it

Demisexual

I'd gotten attached to you, sort of how sticky notes get stuck to walls and notice boards. I got hooked, like you were a fisherman and me, I was the fish on the end of the rod. Connected, even if I didn't want to be. I think we formed a bond in the ponds

I tried to hide it, I didn't understand it. I'd let you ride my imagination though, you're the only one with a ticket to the attraction. Testing out rides, just for your pleasure. I took long to get here, to the top I know. Give me a chance to catch my breath. This feeling, cemented into my body, is making me want you effortlessly.

I'm afraid I'd gotten attached, sort of how sticky notes get stuck to walls and notice boards

Hands

I can be the ice queen but,

in the right hands I am lava girl

F is for friend

It's fine, if every weekend doesn't lead to party shoes and getting tipsy on cheap alcohol. I used to think friendships were about gossiping and sleepovers, now I know they are not

It was 4am in the morning catch ups sat in a car watching the night sky picking each other's brains to pieces. 3pm in the afternoon napping because we somehow both fell asleep at the same time

It was knowing who was always there no matter the situation ahead. It was the "I'm picking you up at 10o'clock be ready" without even knowing if you were even busy

It was the stories without judging, facial expression conversations in a room full of people. Understanding the silence even when I have a voice. Countless insults with fire comebacks like were playing tennis, hit after hit

The "you don't even need to ask I got you".
Everything rolled into one, love in the strangest but ever so fulfilling form

I used to think friendships were about gossiping and sleepovers, how wrong had I been

Soul speaking

You start talking with my soul

And I never know what my replies will be

Freeze Frame

I wish I could freeze this

Put it in a frame and say

This was our moment

Sapiosexual

I dig your soul it speaks so tenderly towards mind. I'd rather you buy me a book from the bookstore, instead of a drink at the bar. I want my imagination to be seduced not my body. Let us be the new naked, where it's our brains that are so open and vulnerable to change of positions. I like to be educated daily. I want to hear you talk about anything like, the stars in the sky, and why we only see them at night. Even if you don't know all the answers

My mind's starving for deep stimulating conversations can you give it?

Falling

I've fallen over a number of times but

as you can see

I keep getting up

I keep on going

I keep on growing

I keep on learning

I keep on proving to myself

Up is where I go next

Myself

I let you know me

In a way that I didn't

Even know myself

At the time

Rather be

I don't mind not being eye candy,

I'd rather be soul food anyway

Good or bad advice?

If it feels right, then it is right

Presence

We could be on opposite streets, or you around the corner. I didn't need to see you. I could feel it... strong, strange, alien. My brain flies into crazy quality, caused by you. I can act like I'm not phased... Reality is you're sending me over board, speeding, fast. We're on a flying boat to neverland, only we never do land

Unlike me

My heart sings when near you,

My heart isn't something that ever sings

Nocturnal Emission

Eyes shut, head back.

All I hear is come for me.

But I'm already there

Times

You're my 4am thought

But also my 4pm

Second thought

You only realise how much you want them to stay, when they are aiming for the door. Leaving. It could be out of your life for a week, a month or forever. Within those moments, in those seconds, it's all you think about. It feels as though the world is going to end. That's when you realise you want them to stay

Thankful

Be thankful for the people you have around you. The people who have helped you in your difficult times, even the ones that have been there throughout the good. Be thankful for these people, for all the times they've picked you up when you were down underground. The ones that have always been loyal to you. The ones who have loved you regardless of flaws. The ones who have put you first without even realising it and been there without question. Keep these types of people close. Very close. They're rare. They're rare

11th Feb

Something clicked

I found someone who understood my silence.

I never wanted to speak again after that day

"You were every single type of material I ever wanted to wear"

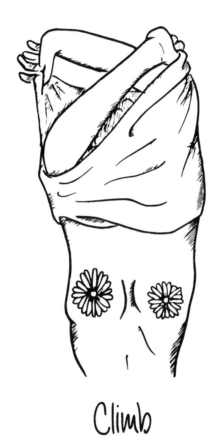

Climb

Flight

You will not find this same love. It's tattooed across you like a seat belt. Holding you in for safety. Protecting you, even when you didn't need protecting. You will not find this same love anywhere else

No more

I start so many things
but along the way
self doubt plants itself into my mind
and then I never finish them

Elutheromania

I wanted to be free

You and I

Out here in the open

Being nothing but open and free

Out here with me

Lights, Camera, attention

It was, a hit and run you've got no insurance for me. But this much I can assure you

I have always been wildfire. You have always been liquid

I had this burning desire, so I allowed you to become my fire place. The home of the blaze, igniting my soul. The becoming of my vulnerability. Like a deer in the wild being chased. So I guess I was the prey, you the predator

Desired hunger, had you feasting like the last supper, with no dining table or cutlery. Just hands, mouth and the floor. Traditionally set. Diving into the deep end of my imagination, while I opened up the gates to my sub-conscious. Are you the archaeologist discovering my hidden treasure, or just someone stealing from it

I had always been mother nature's soil. You had always been the seeds

I was a naked canvas, who allowed you to paint. What were you trying to create of me? Your brush constantly enchanting my canvas. Then you'll step back to admire your new Mona

It wasn't a hit and run. It was a hit, but I think we both missed the beat

Home

Home doesn't have to be a building

with walls, windows and a roof

It could be a person with

a heart, a rib cage and some lungs

Meeting

We never met by accident...

Left and right

You're missing a left rib, that's why I always stay in place on the left side of you. Where Eve was created, so you never felt like apart of you was ever actually missing. Let me snuggle into your side and pretend we don't have to move, that we can stay like this for a lifetime and a few seconds. It's ironic I was your left side because you were my right everything

Choker

Wrapping your fingertips around my neck

You're becoming my natural choker

Submission in the woods

I have gone into the woods, do not search for me.
I don't want to be found, well not yet

The breeze was keeping me cool, while the leaves
stuck to me. I loved the glow that touches me, but
it's spring. The trees they're the richest green I think
I'd ever seen. Like emerald. I can feel the earth
beneath my feet as my shoes touch the ground. I've
got my backpack and a bottle of water. He has a
treehouse and a lantern light. He told me I could
stay the night, so I do

You were here trying to get out, while I was here
trying to get in. I'd gone so far out into the woods
I was no longer on the map trail. How did you even
find me out here? Where the nature of the woods
was welcoming me with open arms. We should trade
places you and I, so I could be here permanently
and you could be where I was in the city with the
lights. I know we only just met but it feels like I've
known you a lifetime

I can hear you so loud in the silence, I wonder how
you perceived me in your mind. You'd been in
solitude for so long, did you remember or know what

togetherness felt like. Before I popped up out of the blue, you started to make me wonder did you turn into a wolf at night. It's just, I never once saw you when it was dark. Maybe you were raised by wolves was that it. If so could I meet them in the night with you, when you ventured around

When the misty fog took over the woods captivating its existence completely. All the wolves howled the most disturbing noise at midnight. The trees they'd sway, the river bank would sing. The wild life would appear from nowhere and I'd be in subtle solitude

The moon shined so bright in the darkness of the night all the monsters turned out to be just trees. When the sunlight came up you were looking for me. Only I was staring right at you. I know we only just met but I feel it deep down like I'm constantly being pulled towards you

He was becoming just like a squirrel with its nuts, so protective and cautious of everything around. I guess he was the squirrel and I was the nuts huh, because he never let me fall, not even once, not even slightly, not at all. He told me I could stay forever with him, so I will

I have gone into the woods only never to return

Your Voice

You speak what's in your heart with a passion indescribable

And they laughed *once*

Now you never speak out

And they ask you why you're so quiet

But they don't understand

Once was all it took

To lock it back up again

Hands II

Your two hands aren't always enough. Even when you hope like hell they can be. Having other hands to help doesn't mean you are weak. You dislike to admit when you need a hand. I get it. At times your own two hands just aren't enough

Cloud 11

Surround yourself around people who see the value inside you. People that remind you of your worth and only want the best for you. They are the people who will lift you when you are falling. They are the ones who keep you in the clouds

The real thoughts

Covering your mind with dirty hands,

Just so clean words won't come out

A taste of connection

Am I still on the tip of your tongue? You dig like you're trying to find golden honey in a beehive. The taste is still the same, I promise. Alphabetting while we're connecting. We're the best kind of art, a painting. My body the canvas, your tongue the paint brush. Am I still on the edge of your conscience? Am I still on the tip of your tongue? The taste is still the same, I promise. It never once changed, so how about this painting?

Hope

I build a house behind that garden wall

I lived in it some days

Eyes closed

I wake up with bruises in the strangest places and wonder how I got them. What adventures have we been undergoing in our dreams lately?

Tropical

Your island aura

Your palm tree flow

Has me spilling tropical juice

Maybe I don't

Maybe I should just allow this to happen

Allow myself to feel the butterflies you put in me. Instead of wondering how they are surviving in me, what colours they are, or how big?

Maybe I don't need to know everything right now, even though I'm forever trying to work every little thing out. From what you're thinking to, did you mean to touch my shoulder like that'? Did you mean to laugh so loud so I could hear you? Did you mean to keep looking at me even after I looked away?

Maybe I don't need to work out how this is going to turn out and just work on going, going forward. Maybe I don't need to figure it all out now, but it's the only thing I want to know. It's the only thing I want to be clear of

What exactly is going on here?

Focus

I don't always use my mind, it uses me sometimes. So wrongly invested into things it never needs to be but, it finds itself straight at that point. I have stopped allowing my mind to use me continuously, but I seem to always realise it when it's too late

Musical instruments

You could be the guitar, I see myself as more of the piano. Every string my fingertips glide on, brings a different sound, out of you. Every key you touch on me, brings a different note to the surface. They call us, the human musical instruments

Unique sounds, not heard often enough, or even at all. Our human noise brings something, out of the ordinary. Something new to this music table. I couldn't get enough of your guitar. And you...couldn't get enough of my piano could you. We're musical instruments, looking for our first show to perform in. So I think we need to start auditioning soon

Screens

Your hand in my hand, my legs over your legs. Sat there with popcorn and cola. I couldn't help but glance into your direction. I could never watch the screens when near you. I loved that you wanted to continuously be touching me. Hands remaining in contact even if I'd pull away. You'd pull me back. It was in that moment I knew where I wanted to be for the rest of my time and all we were doing was sitting in front of the cinema screen

Body parts

He places his lips on yours

His hands around your neck
He can't get enough
Pulling you in closer, tighter

His lips end up on your shoulders
Drawing pictures of hearts

His nose on your hips
Breathing you in
Making your body do flips

His teeth on your back
Taking a bite
Making you arch to his reach

Petal kisses on your belly
Finger tracing along your elbow

He reaches to your legs
Always tangled with his
Two intertwined vines
In a vintage tree

His hands touch private parts

Unlocking
Making you come apart
Your skin is a map for him
He's inside the treasure box
Until he finds the treasure
He's been searching for

Bee sting

I've always known a bee can sting you surprisingly, when your vision was off guard and unfocused. They could pop out of nowhere and attack. I was out here hiding in the caves, because I wanted to be alone, in the wilderness. When you surprisingly stung, and you surely weren't a bee. It was your powerful words that stung me, and not venom

Making me want to know more, more of what your words sounded like. We build a fireplace, just outside the cave, to keep us warm in the night. You'd taken me by surprise out here, where I thought it was only me out here. Turns out, you were here too. Your sting, opened my mind to the possibilities of this world

Love of some sort because of how caring your tone was towards me, without even knowing me long. You guided me on my lonesome adventure, showing me the ropes. Now we travel along these paths together. You've became my personal bee, only your sting never stung me viciously

What they've done

People would make me feel stupid

Then I never wanted to use big words.

I never felt smart enough

To articulate them and explore them

I stayed stuck in a box

Never opening the lid

Or peeping out

Just here wanting more

But never feeling as if

I deserved it

Blindfolded

Blindfold, my eyes but, my soul still reads you, like the back of my hand. Even in the darkest hour, I find light. My hands running through your hair, while you lay there in front of me. I'd watch you, secretly thanking the universe for bringing someone that challenged my mind. We clash, like two separate houses, never wanting to admit our wrong doings

Handcuff my palms but my fingers, they still touch you. Effortless. An electrified feeling for the keeping. I always find my way back to superior. Even blindfolded and handcuffed, I find you

Words

I would most certainly believe your conviction, as if we were sat in a court room. I've already shouted NOT GUILTY way before I know whether you are or not. You're so good with words after all, the way the letters so naturally roll of your subjective tongue. Like skates on a pavement, so free. Causing a sensual sound, one that I now always hear in the background of my mind. Words of 10's, 100's and 1000's

Remembrance

I remember late night drives and drive thrus
New songs and loud voices
Running down paths and slow strolls
Having a sing song in the car
Shoulder naps and TV shows
Neck kisses and shy laughs
That beating heart and a good set of lungs
Picking food and reaching over
Late night conversations and secrets
I remember it all

Hostage

There's someone in your house
There's someone in your home
There's someone in your house

You turn and it's him inside you
Running around moving pictures
Painting walls, redecorating

Touch

It brings me to the edge of every high building

Demanding me to fall to feel

Demanding me to continue to let you touch

Life's a beach

Mistakes happen, but we still find ourselves at the beach front. Letting the water touch our toes while we build sand castles and take in the view

Weighing

Stop holding onto the things that are weighing you down it will not help, they will not take you further than here

Bittersweet

We loved with a love

That was more than just love

I don't think we'll ever

Love someone else

In that exact way

I'm not quite sure if that's

Sweet or bitter

He is

He doesn't like me talking to other people, you see he gets jealous. He. Gets. Jealous. It's okay, that's just him declaring again. He comes as a surprise, I don't know if that's a surprise to me or him. He's contagious, infectious, demanding too. I could be drowning in a pool of emotions, emotions are the only things I can't ever swim casually through. They carry too much feeling, too much uncertainty over me. This is how I would begin to drown; he has to help me help myself but does he?

My heart, it's pumping out of my chest, I'm losing my breath. You don't understand, does that make sense? It's him... Its all him and we both know it, he is the cause, he is the reason. Cuddle me when I say don't because I actually mean the opposite. He doesn't understand, beat my own chest till I'm nearly dead. This is what I do, because of him

I think of negative things that can arise, I could be walking down the street and get hit by a car, maybe I am the car. Or maybe I'll be saved from it, reality sets in and I realise it's all in my head. One by one, they drop only it's not people its all me. Dropping panic into my own veins, like bombs and the stream to the end is a bloody nightmare

The possibility of these day dreams can play on my mind, for days it seems. Making me feel some type of way without really knowing the direction. Why does he do this? Because he loves me? He says he's what I want but reality is, He is not. He is totally the opposite. Over analysing, overthinking so all the simple tasks begin to take a lifetime and a few seconds to complete. When it could have taken less than 5 minutes

He's not here to hurt me, well I hope that's not the case. He is so stubborn, turning the lights on, so I'm the headline of the night. Shining, so of course they all see me. He doesn't understand, I want the obscurity not the limelight. I don't have a performance to give, why does he shine light on me. Now they are waiting for what I'll show them, but I have nothing, I'm full of worry now, he's highlighted me. I love him yes, but he shouldn't be around

I'm on a tightrope, moving forward and also back,

losing balance. When all you have to do is "BALANCE" it's simple. It makes me question if my friends secretly hate me, they laugh at my jokes. I don't understand why when not even I do. I look around like did they laugh. They did. Am I funny? I'm not funny. So yeah, they must secretly hate me. It's weird, they often seem to like me too, more than I do myself some days. I think I have switches inside of myself, only I'm not the one who controls them.

It's him, he touches them at any given time. So I guess it's him who surprises me. He and my mind inside are in a fist fight right now, and he is winning and I am on the ground and they are counting down. He always wins this isn't new. My mind is going at 100mph but look at me I am still. I haven't even moved in 5 seconds, my brain and body don't cooperate together.

Every word you utter to me will be repeated inside and stretched and analysed and re read with different emotions. So I can try and figure out which one you were really saying to me in that text. Yes, even your words in a bubble have me thinking. Ermmmm, how did she exactly say this word.

Ermmmm, was he shouting when he wrote this. I over analyse the time in which you take to reply because I know your phone is in your hand. So yup I guess they don't want to speak to me, or I must just be sooo annoying

Like a maths problem, that you can't work out but you feel the problem. the problem leaves but the feeling it stays, it lingers. I can't work out what 3 minus the problem is, I can't solve the solution or subtract it. He is it. A problem you can't escape

He is anxiety and he loves me, so I guess I love him too

"Most only come for a visit. Kind of how you visit a museum to admire it but not to stay. Not to familiarise yourself and make a home out of it. That wasn't the plan"

Cruise

Glasses

Sometimes you can't even explain what you see in a person, you just see it. Maybe you're the only one that can see it because you are the glasses that allow you to focus properly

The over thinker

Yes, I even over think
My overthinking
This is what I do

Begging

I don't want to beg for this love

I deserve for it to be given naturally

Back here

You come back

And I open up every gateway for you again

I let you visit my safe place and lay within it

With no time of when to leave

I allow your aura to connect with mine again

I let you back here again

And we both know why I'm back here again

Naked

I stripped myself in front of you
Still wearing every bit of my clothing

She is

She is rare

She is so rare

You will begin to look for her

In all of these places

But she will never be found

She is unmatchable

She is rare

But you already knew this

No in-between

They either believe in you or they don't

They either love you or they don't

They either care or they don't

There is never any in-between

Don't allow there to be in-betweens

Two sides

I'm imagining you're both in it

That you're both in the picture, only you're on the boat now. They are still on the deck watching as you glide away

Slightly waving

Pretenders

They aren't all your friends; they don't all want what's best for you. Even if it seems as if they really do. This is where the pretender mode kicks in. Hard to see the genuine and the masked, because they mix within the same water. Protecting their egos, you'll notice them, when it gets tough. Your heart won't always want to believe it, but your mind, your mind will always know and understand. Sometimes these pretenders don't even realise they are pretending, and that's the sad thing. I guess that's just a friend

Soft

I'll always be soft for you, that's the problem. It seemed like you needed holding down, so I held you down. It wasn't a sign of weakness, it was a sign of understanding and I understood you. Not wanting to burden me, but your problems, your words, your anxiety, I took it on hand in hand with my own

I wanted to protect you, I became protective of you, after a while you became so soft for me too.

Soft enough to let the hard layer go, we became so soft. There were no layers left to shield under. I'll always be soft for you, that's the problem my dear, that's the problem

Always

Tell everyone you love, that you'll always love them. You know, loving their imperfections are a part of the process, it makes them who they are. No matter how many times you want to get your hands and wrap them around their heads as if that is the answer. No matter how many times, they get tangled up in their emotions and you start to lose count of them. Tell every one of them that you love them, that you'll always cherish them. You never know when the end is the end and the beginning has really begun

You are

He is not the sun, you are

He is not the stars, you are

He is not the moon, you are

He is not the light, it is you

And this is why he loved you in his darkness

I still can't comprehend how you forgot this

Playing

Trust your gut the first time around

it

isn't

playing

you

Missing

Let them learn to miss you
They'll soon see the way
That they wrapped themselves
Around you for their comfort

Irony

I would have dropped everything

for you,

and in the end

you dropped me

for everything else?

Underground & spotlight

I kidnapped you out of darkness, while I'm somehow still trapped inside. Taking a hold of my limbs and not letting go. Holding me hostage, don't worry I'll be fine. I wasn't beneficial for your bright, not needed like I used to be. Only for your darkness, in the underground

You fled, when my intention with you was never a goodbye. I guess that's the difference between underground and spotlight. Only ones allowed to shine

Grass

Focus on your own grass

stop trying to figure out

how everyone else is growing theirs

Smile

Smile, especially when all you want to do is break down

Just use that last little bit of energy to move those cheeks

Fearing

Leave the fear behind you
stop carrying it with you
wherever you go
You are not what you fear

Moon and return

You could go to the moon and back for someone.
But to them you still forgot to bring back the stars
on your way home

Maybe I'd just go to the moon and stay there. Save
myself the disappointment and ache

Alphabet

If plan A doesn't work its okay

You still have the rest of the alphabet

Missing II

No, they don't put posters up around the town of you. It's because you're not missing in that way. You didn't just one day, not show up at your house. My body, aches with the fact that no one's out looking for you, like I hoped they would. No one around here looks for someone, who isn't actually a missing person. You're missing from the heart, and I think that's a lot worse

I think

You fell in love with the idea, the idea of having someone that got you completely. That was able to understand what you meant even when you didn't speak. You fell in love with the night calls and afternoon meetings. Car rides and sightseeing, passionate kisses and calm helloes. Bold conversations and timid reactions. You fell in love with the constant shoulder, having someone you could protect but also detect. Having someone who knew you just as much as you did yourself

I think you fell in love with everything except me

Distance

We can't be "just friends"
We don't have that in us

Comfortable

Why were they *comfortable* telling you my flaws?

Allowing

You need to remember no one has the power to hurt you

without the permission of yourself

Sad eyes

You're so beautiful, but your eyes, they are so sad, as if you've carried the world on your back with stories of forever's. Words of never's and voices of whoever's been around

Not easy

It is not as easy as opening up your hands

And watching the pain fly away

It is not a caterpillar turning into a butterfly

It doesn't work like this

You can't just let it go like this

It never happens like this

It takes time

It takes patience

If you aren't done feeling

It is okay

No one is telling you to switch off

Lip service

You're not permitted to say a bad word about me, with the same tongue that explored

You

You are stronger than you give yourself credit for

Dangerous scissors

If I've by chance reached for the scissors and cut, you've led me there. You cannot hand someone a pair of sparkly metallic scissors, excepting them to not want to try them out, to see what they really do

Curiosity kills too many cats. If you don't want someone to leave, to flee away from here, stop repeatedly handing them these scissors, they can cut real deep. Chances are, one day they'll try them out to see how different it is with the material cut in twos, threes and fours. These are the most dangerous scissors you can hand someone. Stop handing them out without thinking about what comes next. Everything changes after

Suadade

The days when you do something and the first person you want to tell is the only person who isn't there. Who would have known missing someone could feel like this. As if the rain is pouring down but, none of it is touching you. A sensation that can't be ignored, no matter how you try and pamper it. The absence of their full presence is noticed, the universe still talks about them to you. Only they are no longer right beside you touching shoulders

Colours

Soon enough my colour filled body will be painted black and white. Can't you see the colour change, or the way I'm slowly disappearing into thin air. Can't you notice all the parts of me that are so unlike me now. They are no longer visible, I'm disappearing, how can you not notice that

The Mirror

She's gazing into the mirror on a Tuesday morning. Her face is clear and so make up less. She knows it's only going to last a couple of hours because soon enough it'll be replaced with a sheer cover shine. You know like the ones you see in the magazines? But, his power to devour her was always much stronger than her will to continuously allow him. Covering up for the world she faces daily, on the outside because inside... she's suffocating while he's contemplating what to do next. Leaving her completely terrified even if he doesn't know it just yet. He was ruining her for anyone that was ever to come after. His laughter consistently got the better of him and took the better out of her

Why is this happening? His fingertips press deep into her windpipe. So she's breathless for a moment or two. The littlest touches can wipe her out conclusively. It comes out of nowhere, so it's always an unexpected cause, which is causing her to do what she knows best. Cover it up. Or he'll discover that the outside walls can detect the signs. So he'll hover over her till it's perfected. He's the ultimate time master and he wears her like a wrist watch. He never needed to watch it tick because, she always on the clock. Trying to play it off because she's still in shock that his actions are speaking louder than any words he'd uttered

She's staring in the mirror on a Thursday night with this bloody lip and a bruised shoulder. Was he the beholder of her body? Because he seemed to know all the parts to touch to affect her instead of protect her. She never wants to feel lonely so she'll stay because solitude was a lot worse than suffering pain that she explored. When she should have been dancing in the rain about a man that she loved, who loved her back effortlessly. But the two of them both knew it would happen again. Excusing all his kicking and punching, as love overrules that all. *Apparently.* He says it's because he loves her, but love shouldn't make you ache uncontrollably. It's all nightmares and no dreamville

His knuckles press straight into her check causing her to freeze. While she pleaded for him to "do no more". No one knows what to expect when they are expecting a horror movie to scare them. They just know it will. Only it's a lot worse when it's a real life movie that you're watching. The pain doesn't hurt that much when you don't see it coming. So she turns a blind eye when her back is to him and his front is to her. He was most passionate when he was raging. His passion was in his rage, that's when he loved her the most

Tragedy but only for the mirror to see

Protection

What you can't seem to wrap your head around is that not everyone is going to hurt you. You end up protecting yourself, from how badly you'd been hurt before. Not everyone is going to give you that same feeling. Deep down, you do know this, but you protect yourself from the unknown. The unknown is what scares that soul of yours

Done to an extent that no one even gets the chance to love you. So much protecting, can cause more dismantling than the actual pain had ever caused you. You still deserve to be loved, over and over and over again. That's what you need to remember, you still deserve love. Even after the pain, even after the hurricane and the storm have both passed. You still need a surrounding of affection and love. Don't hide away and think you're protecting yourself by doing so

You were leaving

Part of me could feel you leaving, that same part never did want to believe the truth in the factual situation. "you wouldn't be walking away now would you?"

The day I turned around and you weren't there, I knew. The little signs I chose not to take note of. All those little signs of you leaving, of you stepping away. They were all true

Female

You have gotten through 100% of all the situations you swore would have drowned you out

Why do you think the water is going to come in now?

Hold your head up

Take a deep breath

Centre yourself and swim

Lifetime

My parents aren't together, well at least on my face they are. I've got my father's nose and my mother's eyes. So on me they'll last a lifetime together

Please stay

The only words, that never left this mouth.

Please. My body language was always shouting it at you even when I didn't want it to. **Stay**

If I said it, would it have made a difference? Would you have chosen to stay?

Cover up

I end up making excuses for your excuses and tell everyone my excuses of them

I guess they don't need to know what they don't need to know

Time Zone

It is midnight somewhere,

maybe where you are

I am here and you are there

We are worlds apart,

but somehow together in time

Haunted house

I ran back to the haunted house
Everyone told me not to go back inside
Everyone reminded me of how much it scared me
the first time, and I still went back. I still opened the
door and yes again I am scared. I couldn't even tell
anyone, this is what I feared because I am here
again. Inside the haunted house

Green Eyes

They see your power

They see all you can bring to the table

They see how strong you are

They see how driven you've become

They see that you're never still

And hardly ever quiet

And do you know what, they hate that

Our secrets

The hardest part about having a problem is recognising you have the problem. Imagine your friends are 10's and you, well you were a Victoria sponge. Not the perfect slice, the slice that got cut and then fell apart automatically. Someone still had to take it because, well its cake. That was me. These friends, they'll tell secrets ones that you'll over hear but not be apart of. Ones that they never share because, maybe it's about the boys that they kiss underneath stairs. Fat girl, skinny friends. Sounds familiar? You, you don't kiss boys underneath stairs, those kind of boys are just in yours dreams and your friends, are living these realities. The only things you do underneath stairs is hide away or eat in secret out of fear of being seen and then called "Fat is eating". Then, everyone knows you're eating and you're the talk of the town and for the one reason you never wanted to be the talk of anyone's town or anyone's world. These words stick to me at night and become permanently tattooed into my arms and legs as a reminder to myself

Even when I am hungry, I should not eat! Don't give

them more of a reason to talk. I look in the mirror and all I see is a monster. The monster is me. Hanging over a toilet spilling ingredients. Crying, trying, sighing. Living this kind of life that you don't want to be living. I only felt worthy when... I don't even know. They compare my body to my friends and I don't get why they do this! I am not my friends. It doesn't matter whether I knew who I was here or not. My secret was I went from a size 12 to a size 6, and well I was still fat on the inside. No breakfast, no lunch or dinner just breathing. They were all so proud of my weight loss. Not realising during my weight loss, I had lost so much of myself, literally deteriorating into dust. I remember sitting in the living room, when my friend said "you have an eating disorder don't you" and just like that an elephant joined the room and it was suffocating every single one of us. The elephant in the room brought his friends along for tea and there was no room for words. I was sick off the toxicity

I laughed so much I cried and then I cried so much I laughed again. It was weird. I was weird, I could go days without eating. Blood tests and weigh ins for them to tell me "you are suffering from..." I couldn't see the packet of crisps, for a packet of crisps and not all the fat that's on the label, describing what it was made out of. Making myself feel guilty for wanting a taste, it's a no from me. When my mind wasn't calorie counting, it was balancing the equation of my worth. These words stick to me at night and become permanently tattooed into my arms and legs as a reminder to myself. Body forgive me, I'm sorry for the sin I have subjected you to when you never wanted to take this road. And then it changes over time. And it's because I am shrinking. I was able to shrink myself into water bottles with a camouflage lid. The inside of my body started floating on water. River running. "Your waist is so tiny. What are you doing to get this body?" and you look back at them and you say "ha-ha this, I'm not doing anything" They don't realise what you're doing to get this thin. Your belly rumbles and you hope to god that they didn't hear because you can't, say oh you know just starving myself to be thin

Thin brought me a different sort of attention to being overweight and oversized and over anything else really. I have hands for knives and forks and my body is the food that I do not eat and it's wasting away and I can't remember why I wanted to be accepted by people who didn't even accept themselves. I just wanted to reach happiness, god damn it! I just wanted to feel happy. The problem with this is I thought happiness was a destination I could only reach thin and tired. Until I became thin and tired with no happy in sight

"If they start to see you as second. It's because somewhere along the line, you've allowed them to always be first. So it could never be your title"

Descent

River flowing

The river started flowing

All the trees blowing

They were all going right

They were all on a flight

Out of here I suppose

To a place no one knows

That's how I knew you departed

I'm not sure what we'd started

But now I'm all alone

Standing here on my own

Seated

Some days I'm so inside myself. I never know how to get out. In a room with no windows and no doors

It's just a room with me in it, seated. I never know how to get out of there some days

Left

The day I plucked up enough courage to leave, you'd never even know it, because you had left weeks before me

The worst

It's not you it's me

Miss take

My biggest mistake was allowing you to remain in
my life longer than you had ever deserved to

A broken heart

The removal truck came to take pieces of your heart, without any notice or warning. Never intending on delivering them to the new home. Which could be seen as the new you. Your heart doesn't only get broken by the boy you love, or the girl you love. It can get damaged by a friend, family, a being

Punctured by the feeling of abandonment. The acknowledgement of knowing you weren't worthy enough. When your heart breaks, it can feel like everything inside you has been stolen. Taken while you were held at gun point, and you had no choice but to **give it up**. Left empty

You were giving pieces of your heart, to people not knowing they store those pieces inside of themselves. In pretty gift wrapped boxes. It leaves you, broken with only certain pieces of you. That don't seem to ever stick together neatly enough, to present or want to present to anyone else. You want it hidden and out of view point

But when a boy or girl you love does break your heart. It can tend to feel like cracking of some sort. You can't seem to inhale, without feeling like you're somehow suffocating. And his touch alone can get all the toxic air in your lungs clean. Or her embrace can leave you in an unforgotten trance. Or when your heart breaks you can feel nothing at all

Yes, we know your heart can break for loads of reasons, not just because of the boy or girl you fell in love with. But that feeling is a deadly one

Bittersweet II

Sat right here with you

My head on your chest

You hand on my thigh

And I start to choke up

And you think I'm crazy

But I tell you

Soon this moment will be over

And it'll just be a memory

And then you're quiet too

Closed doors

No

Not every situation needs closure

Stop opening up locked doors

To be faced with the same reality

Good doesn't come from it

Save me from me

It's half 3

I'm sat here

Same thoughts as yesterday

They take over my mind

I am trapped here

In this place unable to move

Holding myself down

Beating myself up

Ripping myself apart

I never know how

I get here

But somehow

At half 3

This is where I am

Leaving

You leave and all I can think is

Am I beautiful enough

Why hadn't I been enough of myself to make you yourself

stay

Mean

I'm mean to myself, I don't even mean to be, it just happens. My own mind torments me. As if I'm living in a recycled world of total meanness. I don't like being mean to me, but it still happens. Until being so mean to me was so much easier than being kind to me

I am my worst enemy at times and I can't help it

Back and fourth

Don't reconnect with toxicity out of the simple fact
that you're lonely

Almost

To have and to hold was as far as we had gotten, there was no death do us part verse. I'm sure I was deteriorating while you were parting. So maybe, it was death do us part. Just not in the normal way, we almost made it, we almost did

Photos

You photograph things you're afraid of losing. I took photographs of you, they were mostly when you were asleep. So you'd never even know it, off guard and still. I guess the secrets out now, because I never showed anyone these photos and I still ended up losing you

Depart

Your circle will get smaller, it's not uncommon. It may not seem like the right thing at the time, but you'll soon be thankful for some people's departures

Leaving II

Every single bone in my body started aching. They could all feel you leaving, why are you leaving. I only wanted you to stay

Thantophobia

You never seemed afraid of losing me, that's the difference. I'm terrified even now you're gone, because losing someone doesn't happen once. It happens over and over, like a cycle. I lose you every time I think of something I want to tell you, and then realise I shouldn't. I lose you when I lay in bed at night and notice another day has gone by and we're growing further away from one another. I lose you in all the silent words and new moments over and over again

Losing you doesn't happen once, it happens every day without you

Blind love

Had you always seen the signs
and chose to ignore all of them?

Russian roulette

I hold a gun to my own head,

and your actions pull the trigger

for me

First time

Left alone with her thoughts again

She can't explain a feeling quite like the ones she is feeling she says

Hard to find words for feelings like these

That's how it begun

The piercing the innocent

The tearing, the destruction

The sad eyes, the cover up

The 'I'm fine' in my 'please *help me*'

Pain added to the already made pain

She found a love for the ripping

That was the scary thing

She started to scare herself

Because she became addicted to the feeling she couldn't quite explain

Deceiving

It's all butterflies in your stomach and googly eyes. Reality is, that they may just be moths, flapping around inside. Moths of anxiety, of not knowing where you stand with the person you want to be completely connected with

Reality

I'm still the one having to pick up the piece's way after the departure. As if I was the one who departed

Trapped

You tend to sugar-coat his affliction for rainbows and hearts. You think remembering good memories will somehow erase all of the bad ones. It never does, they just end up trapped in an undisturbed part of your brain

Hurt is NOT your home

You need to quit breaking your own heart. Trying to conjure up all the reasons why things happen to go wrong, or even why it doesn't go according to how you planned it. Stop making a prison out of yourself for a love, that won't necessarily come the way you hoped. A man in love will do what it takes to keep you, if he wants to. Excuses will always be just excuses. Please don't lose yourself or your worth by going along with a plan, he has for you both. People are meant to enter your world but not all will stay and that's okay. Not all of them are meant to, it will make sense soon, if it doesn't already. Try not to lose balance or forget to shine. Just because he made darkness doesn't mean you live in it. You are light, the darkness is where you shine the brightest. Did you forget that. You're bound to get hurt, it's life it happens but that doesn't mean live inside the hurt. Hurt is not your home, your soul doesn't deserve a permanent key to that house. Stop settling and go and swim, the ocean is waiting for you. Hurt is not your home. So please stop breaking your own heart by holding onto someone who sadly let you go

No Games

He'll say "let's hang" out instead of being straight forward in saying let's go on a date, and then the confusion comes into play. It's so you don't get the 'wrong idea' but the right idea is already inside your head. Seeing as he's asking you to hang or bang or both and all the in-between. The in-between only confuses you more, you'll wonder what is this, are you dating? are you single? So of course you'll want to ask or you do ask? For your own peace of mind, but then, is your mind at peace?

Unseen

You know when you go out detecting, hoping you find exactly what you're looking for. Until you find that thing and wish like hell you can un-see it. The feeling you feel now is exactly how you thought you'd feel it. Only now you're actually feeling it, it's worse. And there's no one to blame but you, you knew what you were getting into

Blank face

I was scared to love, but loved so deeply

So effortlessly and without question

Until question was all you gave me,

And I wanted to continue to hold you like the answer

But you're not the answer are you,

You're just an exclamation mark

That shouldn't have been added on

Leaving III

How did you leaving only make me question my worth. Why can't you see, I was giving you everything to stay. Yet you still aimed for the door, not looking back once

Womanhood

Please stop allowing your womanhood to become his hiding place. Your core isn't somewhere he can keep planting seeds. When he feels like gardening

Please don't make your body the reason why he keeps coming back You're more than that hour glass figure, he keeps taking sips from getting drunk. He should understand this. You shouldn't allow this, but you still will won't you

Words

As you lay there, I hope you remember what every word sounded like. How every sentence rolled off my creative tongue, into your imagination. I hope my words appear on all the pages and the books you read. How my paragraphs had detected feelings to arise to the surface. What do my words sound like when you repeat them, out into the open space? Must be different from how you picture them in your mind. Poetry is a language that I made you become fluent in. I even picture words in your silence. My words are my power, we both know what my words are like. We both know what my words can cause. Words that come out of my eyes, are the only words, I cannot describe

You don't

You don't go back to what broke you the first time. No matter how much you love them. No matter how much they have changed this time around. Your pieces will not be mended here. Your pieces will still remain broken. You don't go back to what broke you the first time. It won't bring you peace, it won't help your broken pieces

Cigarette light

The pain became unbearable

At first, I was fire for your cigarette to be lit

Then I was the astray, the home where you ended them

Both painful

Both still painted in my mind

Difference

My mind knew you wouldn't stay

My body hoped that you would

Pieces

I allowed you to break me down

In hopes that you'd be the one

To put me back together again

How foolish had I been

The gun at arm's length

You won't see the damage, and that's why I have to go. You've already picked your bunch of flowers from my garden. But I need you to say goodbye, before it gets too late

Before there was no one so I lived without a care. Until there was you, that was all I could bare. I thought we'd make endless memories and not end in history. Hold up your gun and let me go at arm's length

Excuses

Their number one excuse is you're too much.

Do not believe this

You are never too much for someone who cannot get enough of you. They will try drumming these excuses into your conscious, you chose to not believe

Medication

When giving them a taste of their medicine

Why do they get upset

When they're the ones who created it

Losing game

Losing a woman who was willing to love you to the death is a pain you'll only feel when you're mature enough to understand it

Tired

She'll get tired

She'll soon leave without explanation

Because she'll become fed up

Fed up of defending you

Defending you to everyone who saw what she couldn't see

This woman will walk away, with pain in her heart but the realisation that she deserved better. That she was better than the unneeded pain you were causing and that she was allowing, because she was so in love. That she would rather stay there and feel terrible than lose you, because she used to think losing you was the worst outcome

She'll get tired

She'll soon leave without explanation

Because she'll become fed up

Fed up of constantly defending you

Defending you to everyone who saw what she couldn't see in you

The truth

Do you?

You make so much effort to get no effort in return

And you think that's what you deserve?

The protector

The heart is so powerful

For it can break a million times

and still be the only thing keeping you alive

Happening

We spend so much of our time focusing on what we don't want to happen. Instead of putting our energy into what we do want. Then wonder why it doesn't go according to plan. When our plan subconsciously wasn't for it to work. Trust the universe it understands you

Selfish

I was needed when you needed a boost of happy.
Then you became happy and gave your happiness
to someone else

Prospective

How they leave you explains all the unanswered
questions. When you're ready you'll get them

Too late

They will realise all the things you've done when you are no longer there. They will realise your uniqueness when they no longer have it near them. When you are gone they will realise too late

First class

She will always be the type of woman you go to
war with and not against

Difference II

There is a difference between someone who's happy for you, and someone who just wants to know what's happening for you

Leave

Sometimes you're just meant to help people in the hardship of their life and then watch them leave

I know, but it's okay

I know you wanted to be with me, some place inside of you did. On those days we'd drive around the city going anywhere, with no destination but always finding a destination to stay in. To be in, to love in, to feel in. The times we'd go to the sea side and glide our feet along the pebbles, throwing them into the water hoping that we'd make them skip. The only thing skipping was our hearts. Hand in hand talking about what we wanted to do with our life. When we weren't doing anything with our lives at that point in time, other than standing side by side. Week after week after week. Never getting tired of each other's existence. 365+2. You'd pull me closer to the point we were practically breathing for each other. I'd hold you tighter, afraid that one day this would all stop and we'd both be left with memories. Memories of what we meant to each other and what we could have become. I know you, maybe I should say I knew you now instead. Because things change and people grow and love ends. Love begins and love dies and starts all over again. But I knew you like the back of my hand. Off by heart like the paragraphs learnt for plays. I can't pretend that this wasn't real, I can't pretend that this makes sense now. Some place inside of you understands this. Some place inside of you gets every word. Somewhere along this path we became torches for each other and it was us against the world. It was us against everything. We had the world at our feet and we planned to travel it, and conquer it, and slay it and make it our bitch. But this is life and things change, and people change. We grow and we break and we tear and we build and we get knocked down and we try and get back up and get knocked down again. And we trust and get let down and we trust again, just for the sake of it. This changed. I can no longer allow myself to be played like an instrument in your personal show. I don't regret you for the world, though. I'm not sure why certain things turn out the way they do. There has to be a deeper plan or a deeper meaning than what we are told. I'll wait for that. Alone. I know you wanted to be with me, some place inside of you did, but it's okay. You don't ever have to admit this to me. Please remember I knew you, probably better than you knew yourself some days. That is enough for me now, that is enough, this is enough and it's okay

Road signs

He claimed that he loved you to hit it

Then he hit the road

Give in

You deserve the same love you are so desperately willing to give out. Please learn to love yourself, always in all ways

If your heart

If your heart is to get broken, it doesn't mean run away from love, maybe run on the bridges. The ones that are so high up your guard doesn't need to be. Walk around on it for a while, but not come back to reality soon, I promise you love will find you some day. Maybe it just wasn't meant for today. That doesn't mean cupid skipped you. Today just isn't your day

Nono

If you cannot see my worth

I will not be a constant reminder

None

There was no fight

There was no out of breath signs

There was no heavy breathing

There was no panic

There was no realisation

It was just you saying don't leave

When your body said just go

Dear heart

Listen to me please

Stop feeling for a while

I can't take this pain

I don't want anyone to see this pain

So if you stop feeling for a while

Maybe it'll go away

Maybe they won't notice me breaking

Maybe they'll think I'm okay

Be on my side for a while

Listen to me please

Stop feeling for a while

Free water

I don't want watered down promises
I don't deserve watered down promises
Don't bring me watered down love
And think I can survive on that
I don't want this, I don't deserve that

Letting

I didn't want to let go
I didn't want you moving on without me
So I packed my suitcases and followed you here
I compromised myself in the hopes that
it would make you want me more

Me, myself and I love you's

I was selfish for thinking that me wanting you to love me, meant that you actually had to. It didn't, it didn't mean anything at all. I'd always wanted unconditional love, and always got semi, half-hearted love, I'm not sure love, maybe later love, someday love, it's not you it's me love, on a tightrope love. All types of love but never, unconditional. I know it was wishful having the thought you could love me unconditionally, but I still pray that you do. I was selfish for thinking that me wanting you to love me, meant that you actually had to

The letter that will never be posted

Will it ever be enough; will I ever feel like home to you? Was I ever home to you? I sat here thinking to myself, does your body feel as cold as mine does when you're not here. What is it like when I am near? Do you have sleepless nights thinking of me? Me on you, you on me. Next to you, by your side? I've always wanted to be home to a person. I was just wondering am I your home? Had I ever been your home? Will I ever be your home in the human form? What is it like when I am next to you? For me it feels like the earth is opening up and rain and thunder and the storm and all these little things that don't really make sense are happening all at once

Losing

They never explained what this would feel like.

Losing a lover that was also your best friend. You lose the shy smirks, the petal kisses that decorate your spine. The love bites that are painted across your shoulders and neck. You lose the butterflies in your stomach, they are exchanged for something empty. You lose the shoulder you'd lean on, the person who hears your endless stories, your dreams and what ifs. Who wipes the tears and knows what you're saying without you saying a word. The person who knows the difference in your silences. When the only one you wanted to tell about this person departing is the best friend who is departing what happens then? You know the person you loved for a lifetime before you wanted to spend the rest of your lifetime with them. They never explained what it would feel like losing your best friend who was also your lover, I'm learning what it feels like

Open apology from heart to mind

I'm sorry, I took over so dramatically. I was just wishing for something different this time around. I was praying that it would out. The truth is going back to who hurt you the first time isn't ever a good idea. You never will heal naturally in this place. You will become locked in the same trap again, deeper this time. You'll be so blinded by the lies and the red flags. You'll condition yourself into seeing them as something completely different

You will try to figure out ways to solve it, you'll blame their misunderstanding and neglect of you on yourself. You may have even started to believe that you can't do better than them. That you'll become alone forever so you settle for what bullshit they throw out to you. You accept it and you catch it with open arms and call it love. This is not love, this is disrespect. This is selfishness. This is you trying to change someone's colours. When they have been painted in so many different ways. They had to open up a gallery to store them all.

I apologise for never listening clearly enough when you were constantly screaming it at me. You can do better than this

"I deserve me"

Landing

Learn it

Learn to be comfortable in everything that makes you uncomfortable

This is how you grow out

This is the beginning of your landing

This is where the pilot lets you go

Never ever

Don't allow them to become comfortable with disrespecting you. They'll think that you accept being treated this way

Green grass

If the grass is greener on the other side for you, go there. I'm too busy competing with who I was yesterday to even think about competing with anyone else

No one

I don't trust anyone with my heart
Not even myself

Mingle

You become like the 5 closest people to you, make sure they are not giving off the energy you don't wish to mingle with. If they do ask yourself

"Do I want to be anything like that?"

Not guilty

Don't feel guilty for walking away from an aura you can't run with. Your soul only deserves the best

Mama

My mother once said to me, whatever is meant to be or whatever is meant to happen. Always will. It's not always down to you, sometimes you have no control over anything

Yourself

Speak like you LOVE yourself

Act like you LOVE yourself

Move like you LOVE yourself

Embrace that you LOVE yourself

Because you are WORTH loving

Always

Losing and Loss

We lose people, not because we no longer care. It's the fact we care too much and they no longer do. We don't deserve to be playing a 2 player game when were the only ones participating in it

This time don't be dumb

I'm tired of you letting them get to you, allowing them to affect your moods. There is a difference between people needing your help and them taking the piss. Please don't be dumb this time, your heart is made of gold and these people don't deserve your expensive devotion to them. Choose wisely, or you'll end up with continuous disappointment. They'll start to get used to using you, by no means change how you are for people. Just please don't be dumb this time

Back

What is meant to be will always find its way back
to the surface. No matter how many plane rides
away you may have taken. There's a plane boarding
to take you right back

Yourself II

Do not expect anyone to love you

If you can't find it within you to love yourself.

It starts and ends with you

Re mine

I have to be a constant reminder to myself, I'm worth too much and not too little. The heart does hurt, and the pain is painful, but I'm worth too much to pretend I'm not

Lesson

When your mouth is closed

And your eyes are wide open

You tend to learn things

You didn't need to attend school to learn

Losing and Loss II

We lose people because we close ourselves off from the world, ask to be left alone. Then get upset, confused, rattled when that exact thing happens. Deep down you wanted them to stay longer

Hold you tighter

But they couldn't hear the **stay** in your **go**

Worth it

He isn't worth the tears. Remember who you were before he came along, go be that person again. She deserves you

The world

I've always had the world within my heart. Within my being, it's just us women. We tend to get manipulated into thinking, we had to go in search of something. Truth is, that something was always inside of us. We are a world within our own self. Some just take longer to recognise that. Learn to love your world. Without having to allow someone else, to justify it for you. Your world is strong. Your world is solid. Be your world, for yourself first

Watch

Keep your eyes open for every time they don't clap when you're winning. It may seem like a minor trait, but the meaning is deeper

Returning

They will come back, every single one of them. Like a pattern or a map trial

They had a coffee break, or a cigarette break and needed the air. They got off those planes and vacated out of here. To somewhere new, somewhere that no one knew their name, or their face or their story. They're blank people in the places that they travelled to. They all left with hopes of returning one day. I know you never pictured them all returning, but they all come back. A week, a month, a year, some years later. But they will all come back to here

You already know

Someone who can't appreciate

or understand your worth

doesn't deserve it

You already know this

Queen

Remember you are a queen, even without a king. You are most definitely still a QUEEN

Give and receive

Some people only give to receive, and if you are one of those, people. I'd rather you never give me a thing

You are

You are beautiful

You are alive

You are breathing

You are magic

You are blessed

How could you ever forget that?

Youth Adolescent

If I could tell my younger self something, it would be love doesn't kill you like you thought it once would

If I could tell my older self something it would be keep going you're meant to wait for it to feel completely real again. Or maybe it now does

For her, for my mother

I'm sorry I shut you out

I let the world get on top of me

I was just trying to work it out alone

I become a different world

But you were the universe

The Brush

Dads never know how to apologise when they are wrong

They never want to admit

They just brush it off

But we want the apology

We want the

You're right

I was wrong

But we never get that

We just get the brush

Gifted

It's okay, life once gifted me with paint

When I only had paint brushes

No settling

Do not settle just because you've waited this long.
There was a reason then, and there's a reason now.
Do not settle continue to swim

No

Don't feel bad for saying it. At times it's needed it doesn't make you a bad person. You don't even need to explain yourself for the times that you do say no. Saying no is enough, so don't feel guilty for it

Ify

I forgive you

For breaking my heart

For walking away

For loving me less than I loved you

I forgive you

For all of above

Most importantly

For my self

Friendly reminder

Always be you, someone could be getting inspired by you or need a you around. Promise me you'll never stop being you. Someone out there needs exactly what you are giving. Be that rainbow on a cloudy day. Positivity comes from believing, so believing is what you have to do. That all comes from loving and embracing yourself, with admiration. Negativity cannot win, we can't let it

Power

You are more than the shoulders they lean on, more than the lips they kissed, when theirs become lonely to the air, brushing past them. More than the streets you were scared of going down. You are more than the voices inside your head that made you think you were going crazy. More than their wake up call from reality, when they are forever hitting snooze

You are more than the people you walked away from, the people who treated you wrong, the lies and their exits. A thousand mistakes and a hundred wrongs. A million rights and a billion turns. You have always been more than just skin and bones and a soul that sings. More than where your parents come from, and the stories they tell you

You are you that alone is your power. You are the electric that you think you need, to face the world. You are more than you can imagine. You always have been

Rebel

I felt like a rebel

When I started loving myself

With every fiber in my being

As if I was never meant to

Planted

Don't be afraid to bloom

Don't be afraid to stand out

They planted you then made it rain

What were they expecting

Other than for you to grow up

Real love

The world has tried to break me down,

But god just built me straight back up

Stronger than ever

Deserving of

You deserve the world and he wasn't willing to even give you a tiny piece of his. Why are you still lingering around? Giving him your world, giving him your all

Another try

I have yet again walked into it

I came here willing to try harder

Willing to try and make this work for real

The two of us together

It could have been a beautiful novel

Of love, returning and bitter sweet chaos

Reality sets in and it reminds me

My hopes are not always what will happen

My dreams are just dreams sometimes,

And you were stuck here with the thoughts of never going further in that way,

But further in every other

Understand

You are powerful with or without the people you love

Last time

I settled for okay, instead of perfect or fantastic or magnificent or lovely or loving or understanding. I was happily settling for okay, because you made it feel good enough. I had to learn how to swim again, how to not drown myself in constant sorrow. To pick myself up. Nine times. I had to remind myself this was not the end of love. That I was bigger than your love. That I was better than your love. That I was the love that I needed

How could I not know your okay love, was ever so mediocre. How could I not know that your inconsistent love for me, was not for me to keep and hold on to. As if it was the best kind of love I was ever going to receive. I am love. How could I not remember that someone like you, could never give me the sort of love I deserved. How did I even think someone like you could possibility or even ever give me less than what I am

You see, loving me was the first thing I felt great at
After losing you for the last time

Yourself III

You deserve yourself

You deserve the love you want to feel

You deserve all the good coming your way

You yourself deserve yourself

You yourself are not asking for too much

Excuses II

Stop making excuses for him, stop hearing his excuses knowing what they mean and defending him, because you think you can't live without him! Remember you once didn't know him and you were doing just fine

You are II

You are gold

You are magic

You are these things yet you still have this doubt within yourself that you can't be loved. When all you radiate is love, there's no reason it won't come back to you

You are magic

You are gold

Battle field

You're there with a sword fighting

Fighting for these people

Coming to their rescue

Being the knight in shining armour

But who's fighting for you?

Who's at your battlefield?

Tell me who's there on your field

With fists and swords and armour

Pain

I stayed in bed and cried all day

Then I done it again the next day

I let the pain hurt

I let the pain come

I let the pain take over

But only for a while

Stop

Stop taking care of everyone but your own damn self. You come first. Stop forgetting about number 1

That is, you just in case you've forgotten again

Fighter

Who fights for me in the end?

God

I put my trust in his hands

He's never let me down once

Wait

It takes an amazing person to love a girl like you. Do not settle for anything other than that amazing person

Where?

Where does all the love go?

Do I keep it, or do you take it with you?

Do I gift wrap it in delicate tissue paper?

Does it then become yours?

Do I have it forever?

What happens to love after we part ways?

I don't want it to just be everywhere

I need to know, where does it go after here?

Who takes it with them?

Me or you?

Where do all these feeling go?

Where will the next home be?

Where does all the love go after here?

Not you

You have scars, you have wounds
You get hurt, you get broken
But these things are not YOU
You are so much more than this

Flaws

Wear your flaws with pride like it's royalty and everyone around you will start to address it that same way

Please Stop

Your self-worth is expensive

Please stop discounting it to people

Who can't afford the original price

29

I reach but we're already touching

Skin to skin

You rub and I am out

I'm a genie, your wish is my command

And this begins the exploring

But I am the one demanding

On my untouched daises

29 petal kisses

Your hands they're placed

Placed on my delicate parts

Parts that you discover

Parts that you attract

Parts that you open

Parts that you make come

Apart and drip like honey

Hand in hand

Tighter closer

You make me react

Mind to mind

Body and soul

I make you react

But I am taken away with the wind

Or am I taken away with your mind

You do this thing with your lips

I do this thing with my hips

This is how we begin on 29

When I say

Is it actually playing or is it in my head. When I say in my head, what I'm saying is that song. When I say that song, I mean 'plotting' or do I mean 'closed doors' because one was mine and one was yours. Some days it's like the big bang, all things loud and chaotic. Others it's a whisper, as if school girls are telling tells in classrooms. Classrooms are where we met and it's crazy because we ended up in car parks

The car parks only had you and me in them at 2am empty and bare. They're not as lively as classrooms filled with noise and disruption. When I say car parks, what I mean is anyplace where we'd stop half way on our journeys of anywhere. We had emotions for hands and feet, when I say emotions I mean words, and when I say words I mean all the feelings, because our mouths never did much talking

Talking is evidentially how this all started out, not that talking was the root. We didn't need to talk to understand each other, when I say understand. I guess that much is self explanatory but somehow a fire started. When I say fire what I really mean is the misunderstanding, the miscommunication, the breaking point. Rewinding before this, it had been epic, it was everything and it was my everything. It had meant everything to me, when I say everything I mean worldwide. As that is bigger than my arms can reach, so you can only imagine the width

But yes the fire started and it was blazing hot, it was uncontrollably happening. No matter how much water I tried to spray onto it, nothing was bringing it down to calm. When I say water, what I really mean is my attempts to make it work

It is not easy to leave you in abandoned places but here in the car park is where I have to leave you. When I say car park, what I'm saying is anywhere I go from here, I can no longer take you with me. I've been taking you on car rides and walks and shopping trips and mountains and rivers. I can no longer have you as a tag along attached to my soul. When I say this, what I mean is I will always love you just from a far

Mirror repeat

I am beautiful

I am powerful

I am enough

I am a queen

I am enough

I can never forget this

I have installed it into my permanent memory

I am enough

I am enough

I can never forget this

For them, **my** family

Thank you for your continuous belief in me and my dreams and my craft

Without every single one of you, this would have never happened

For them, **my** best friends

Thank you

For listening

For understanding my silence

For helping me

For protecting me

For your shoulders

For your ears

For your words

For your courage

For your hearts

For your belief

I am **so** much stronger because of you all

For her, **my** illustrator

Nahlah Alsree thank you

For your amazing illustrations

throughout this book

You've made it so much easier

for me and you've brought

my visions to **life**

I am ever so grateful

for your time and dedication

For you, **my** readers

Thank you for inspiring me

Thank you for supporting me

I am so grateful for you all

Every single one of you

For you, **my** muse

Here are words

"If you aren't a priority in your own life then you're living it wrong"

Undo your seat belts

I hope this book holds a place in the bookshelf of your soul

Writing has taught me how to be at peace with myself, and how to live in the now. A more content and lively place, because when you actually stop and take a deep breath. You start to realise life is pretty amazing. We have the pleasure of experiencing it in the ways that we wish to

Don't cheat yourself out of this, never allow anyone to make you feel bad, for not doing all the things they'll do along the way. You were not created for their purpose. You are here for you, do what lights *your* soul up. What doesn't kill you will bring out the power in you. Your happiness has and always will count

Your self-worth and value should, always be kept high and not given out freely to people, who have no clue how they are meant to correctly handle it

With my **whole heart,** thank you. You've arrived here safe and sound at this destination and that was all I wanted. Because of you I know I have never been alone. You have helped me by just coming along on this flight with me

Thank You

Instagram: @Denelleblack

Email: denelleblack@gmail.com

Facebook: Denelle Black

Printed in Great Britain
by Amazon